SHIFT CONSCIOUSNESS, CHANGE EVERYTHING!

Ed Oakley

Marjorie,
Congratulations for the way you're soaring — in Consciousness and Life!

Love you!

Ed Oakley ☺
10/28/13

What People Are Saying about
SHIFT CONSCIOUSNESS, CHANGE EVERYTHING! Part 1

Whether we admit it out loud or not, we all know there is a level of awareness or understanding about our existence that we're missing out on. There is something else. Our suspicion is that this 'other' level is so powerful that maybe we shouldn't be messing with it. Well don't tell that to Ed Oakley. In this new book he's managed to pry open the door to this new world of possibilities just enough for us to peek in. Indeed it will frighten some...but for those of us who want to breakthrough the gravity of our current mindset to the weightlessness of our highest potential this book is a welcomed guide.

Ian Percy,
Author of *Going Deep* and
The Profitable Power of Purpose

I've known "of" Ed Oakley for many years and have followed his great writing on the subject of leadership and have only "actually" known him for a few months.

I had the opportunity to have a very deep and personal conversation with him recently and it led me to an awareness about awareness. A few more conversations and introspection have brought me to a place that I wasn't sure I would ever be—experiencing a clarity unlike anything I've known before.

Only last week, I was getting an even clearer view of my level of awareness and really experienced a breakthrough moment after a circumstance occurred that at a glance would not think it was something that affected me directly. Ed and I spoke after this event, and he was able to demonstrate that he could detect that shift and how it was affecting me—not actually knowing what the situation was.

Fear, pain, worry, and conflict have a new place in my life and are serving me now more as tools for growth rather that barriers holding me back from the success that I know is Divinely orchestrated and waiting for me to simply latch on to and move to the next level!

This book has really helped me to understand what all of this means and how anyone can breakthrough to influence and significance.

Mark Crowley,
Radio Host and Producer

"We use 10% of our brain" ~the Objective, Scientific, Rational, Causative aspect that created all we enjoy today.

The other 90% is the Wisdom part: the Subjective, Intuitive, Permitting, Only-Experienced aspect of our brain and life, that few individuals rarely experience. In this brief book, Ed Oakley masterfully opens wide the door to our Whole Brain and Being to function fully alive in both Objective and Subjective dimensions.

Dr. Ed Carlson,
Founder of Core Health

SHIFT CONSCIOUSNESS, CHANGE EVERYTHING! is a monumentally important contribution to the literature on consciousness and consciousness studies/research. It's also a major advance forward in the conscious/mindful leadership movement. Never before has it been possible for "ordinary people" to have the effect of consciously causing someone to move past the shift point (Threshold of Influence™) on David Hawkin's Map of Consciousness scale.

Ed has clearly demonstrated this is possible—not only possible, but happening right now!—and that it can happen on a massive scale. I highly recommend *SHIFT CONSCIOUSNESS, CHANGE EVERYTHING!* to anyone who is truly interested in advancing their own personal growth, and particularly recommend it to organizational leaders who recognize that leadership of business, non-profits, and governments must change if we are to heal societies and the planet.

Don McCrea, Ph.D.

Co-author of *Enlightened Leadership: Getting to the Heart of Change*

SHIFT CONSCIOUSNESS, CHANGE EVERYTHING!

Part 1: Make the Breakthrough

Ed Oakley

© 2013 by Enlightened Leadership Publications

All rights reserved. No portion of this book may be reproduced, stored in a retrieval system, or transmitted in any form or by any means—electronic, mechanical, photocopy, recording, scanning, or other—except for brief quotations in critical reviews or articles, without the prior written permission of the publisher.

Published in Denver, Colorado, by Enlightened Leadership Publications, wholly owned by Enlightened Leadership Solutions, Inc.

ISBN: 978-1890088033

To my dear wife, Jonette Crowley, who put up with so much over the years before finally getting the husband she was looking for— thanks to the consciousness shifts discussed herein.

Contents

Introduction	7
Who Am I?	11
What's in This for You?	15
Map of Consciousness	19
Why Would I Want to Go to India?	25
At Oneness University	29
Is This Religious?	33
Some Amazing Gifts I Received	35
Breakthrough Research on the Flights Home	39
Back Home from My Transformational Experience	45
The Surprises Continue	47
The Perfect Test Labs	49
An Amazing Experience	53

When Jim Came Home	55
Did Those Psychological Suffering and Other Numbers Stay at Zero?	57
What About the Other Experimenters?	59
Maybe an Even Bigger Factor	63
A Breakthrough Realization	65
I'm Supposed to Do What?	69
Oh, I Forgot to Wear My Reading Glasses	73
How Am I Doing All These "Tests?"	75
My Ultimate Test of the Pendulum	83
So, How Do You Break Through the Threshold of Influence?	87
What's All This Got to Do With Transforming Your Life?	99
Last Minute Comment	111
Appendix	113
Index	119
About the Author	121
Where to Find More Info	123
Other Books by Ed Oakley	124

Introduction

For over 25 years, we've been teaching Enlightened Leadership to people in 68 countries. In fact, Doug Krug and I wrote the book, "Enlightened Leadership: Getting to the *Heart* of Change," and it has been a huge best-seller. It is still available as a Simon & Schuster softcover, as well as on Kindle as an ebook.

Our work has been gratifying and effective, as significant numbers of people on projects and in organizations shifted how they worked with people. Just as important as organizational results clients have had are the many personal breakthroughs in relationships, family and life in general.

Regardless of their personal or organizational roles, individuals and teams used our tools like Effective Questions™, Forward Focus™, 5 Action Steps for Breakthrough Results™, Framework for Leadership™, Personal DNA™ and numerous others. When they did that, family and team members responded and breakthrough results, higher engagement, and greatly enhanced relationships resulted. All of our previous books have shared many examples of significant successes for both organizations and individuals. We pride ourselves in the simplicity, practicality and effectiveness of our tools, concepts and processes.

And we've always said it's not so much what you do but how you do it, or a level deeper, "where you 'come from'" in the process of doing it. Are you coming from trying to use these tools to merely solve the personal problem? Or is there a deeper part of you that wants to honor all the parties in the process, to develop more fulfilling relationships, to create an environment that naturally brings out the best in everyone? That's a huge difference, and that's a fundamental consciousness issue.

There's an irony here. As creator/author of many of the excellent tools of Enlightened Leadership, I now realize that a person whose consciousness is above a certain level doesn't need them. Why? Because people above that breakthrough level of consciousness already come from a pure intention that naturally drives the right behavior—the kind of behavior that brings out the best in everyone around them.

So, there is really good news here. At a time when we desperately need to change behaviors on the planet so we'll stop destroying the Earth and each other, we have a way to do

Introduction

it. We can DIRECTLY raise the consciousness of people whatever their roles in life. Why now? Because for the first time in the history of human civilization, we can.

This book is about how we've helped thirty-eight people (at this writing) raise their consciousness beyond what I am calling the Threshold of Influence™. We discuss the benefits they are receiving as well as different ways you can cross this threshold too. Crossing that threshold is a personal breakthrough that puts you on a whole new growth curve that will transform your life in ways you probably cannot even imagine now.

This book is a work in progress. You'll find new and updated information at:

http://www.enleadership.com/breakthrough/shift.

Register now while you're thinking about it!

Who Am I?

I'm an integrator. Over the years I've learned that possibly my best talent is taking concepts, perspectives, ideas and tools from a variety of sources and integrating them into simple, powerful, practical ways of dealing with complex situations. This work is no different. A number of concepts, perspectives and tools will be utilized to address what I consider to be extremely important today—directly raising our consciousness for the benefit of ourselves and all those we influence.

One thing *is* different about this situation. I found myself in a personal development process, and somehow, I felt there was something significant about it. But I didn't know what. I felt strongly though that I should keep extensive records. You'll see significant chunks of those as we move forward. My hope is this data will help at least some of you better understand what happened, what is happening, and what can happen to you.

The focus of this book is about consciousness, and specifically raising your consciousness for your personal benefit and that of all those you touch. It's about the many benefits you'll gain by doing so. Over a very short period of time, I've had tremendous insights about this topic and have validated them to my standards, which we'll discuss. I've literally been bombarded with this exciting information at virtually every turn in my life.

It's not surprising that it has happened, as I've just been through a significant shift in my own consciousness—which we all can do. There is nothing special about me in this. It has everything to do with the dramatic and critical transformation of mankind's consciousness that hit a critical mass late last year and is now accelerating. Remember all the discussions and predictions around December 21, 2012? While some of the predictions were misguided, it did signal a tipping point of a new era where rapidly rising consciousness is the norm—for the first time in history to my knowledge.

And with such a shift, I'm finding that it is typical, even expected, to have whole new perspectives and ideas about the areas of expertise you have already developed. Just like the consciousness jump, the awareness and creativity goes rapidly to new levels. It's like you suddenly have access to a whole new

Universal data base of information around your expertise that was never available before.

That access takes you to dramatic new levels of personal and professional effectiveness.

What's in This for You?

Let me share some benefits I personally achieved from this work that are available to you, too.

I did a pre-test of the following emotional/psychological factors before beginning the work. Later in the book we'll go into more detail about each of them, but just see how you relate to where I was on April 1st of 2013. The scale is 0 - 100%.

Psychological Suffering - 95%. I know. Scary.

Fear of Failure

Fear of Rejection

Fear of the Future

Fear of Death. Average score 20% across the four.

Mental Conflict - 36%

Hurt - 20%

Dissatisfaction - 22%

Being Judgmental - 26%

Having Attachments - 32%

Pleasure-seeking (in a way that consumes your effectiveness) - 46%. Oops.

Day-dreaming (waste of energy) - 25%

Living Up to an Image - 75%. Ouch!

Trying to Change Who I Am - 56%

Worry - 45%.

Mind Chatter - Oh yeah! 52%

Boredom & Loneliness - 7%.

Feeling Empty Inside - 16%

Craving (a big step up from simple desire) - 41%

Need for Permanence - 36%

Seeking Perfection - 6%.

Living Outside of the Present (wasting energy, focus, etc.) - 36%

Understanding Who I Am - 24%. Wow, you want this one high!

Many of these numbers were shocking to me. The good news is that every one of them improved dramatically with my consciousness shift, and continue to improve to this day.

What's in it for you is to do the same for yourself – regardless of your starting numbers.

What's in This for You?

The breakthrough numbers are shared later in this book.

We're discovering new insights about this research constantly. Register now for free ongoing updates at http://www.enleadership.com/breakthrough/shift.

Map of Consciousness

That brings up the first concept that will be integrated into this work. In his book introduced about ten years ago, *Power vs Force*, David Hawkins, MD, introduced his Map of Consciousness, a logarithmic scale from 1-1,000, which he used to discuss the consciousness of people and the characteristics at each level.

The level of 1 is barely alive, and the level of 1,000 is Christ, Buddha, Krishna Consciousness. I capitalize because it doesn't get higher than that, and that's a level of behaviors and reverence to which we would all do well to aspire. Dr. Hawkins estimated that 80% of the people on Earth are actually at 200 or below, which is negative, contracting, energy "taking" consciousness. For instance, Hitler calibrated at 175. Scary, huh?

See Appendix for how to find information about Dr. Hawkins.

Shift Consciousness, Change Everything!

The subtitle of Dr. Hawkins' book is "The Hidden Determinants of Human Behavior." Does that get your attention after seeing where Hitler was? Your level of consciousness determines behavior. How many times have you tried to change someone's behavior to no avail? If their consciousness hasn't changed, their behavior is not likely to change either. Consciousness determines behavior.

Let's make it more personal. How many times have you tried to change your own behavior without long term success?

Fortunately, as you go higher and higher up the consciousness scale, your behaviors naturally shift more and more for the greater good of all and become less and less selfish. This is very important. Hawkins estimates that one person calibrating at a consciousness level of 500 offsets the negativity of 750,000 people below 200.

Did increasing your consciousness just take a new significance? We hope so! The key to really impacting the average consciousness on the planet is to raise the consciousness of those already at reasonably high levels.

What happens to people at the higher levels is that they naturally provide leadership. This has nothing to do with position or authority. An individual's "Influence Power™" increases exponentially as they move up the scale. Influence is what leadership is all about. You've probably had an experience of a person in a "low level" role who influenced you in a positive way.

This book and the series to follow will most likely appeal to people with MOC (Map of Consciousness) levels of 590 to 699. Frankly, if you've gotten this far, you're probably in that range. We can measure it for you if you like. See Appendix.

That range is significant because that is where we tend to find so many people who are ready and eager to do what it takes to take their personal and professional effectiveness to new levels. Because of their consciousness level, they are naturally eager to break through the old limitations. They are also people who will be the most openminded, the most willing to consider new perspectives and ideas.

This relatively small range of MOC also represents a limited number of people. This book is not focused on the masses, but more on those people who can and will most easily and naturally make a bigger contribution to our society through their influence.

As one's effectiveness, clarity and influence increase through shifts in consciousness, she or he naturally tend to provide more leadership—regardless of their roles in life. When I use the word leadership in this book, I am specifically talking about the kind of leadership that contributes to families, people, work and society, and makes a positive difference wherever they are. They add to our society instead of take away from it, and they are often eager to do more.

Threshold of Influence™ is addressed in this book. While it's relatively easy to move in consciousness from 465 to 470 or from 551 to 555, there is an important glass ceiling that awaits us when we reach 599. This is what we're calling Threshold of Influence. I estimate that 52% of western society business leaders are stuck just below this Threshold of Influence. Many others are even below that!

Only about 5% of those leaders are above the Threshold of Influence (over 600). This is where we need more leaders. This is where individuals will make the greatest difference due to their positive influence. They are also increasingly effective, positive and supportive of their people, their families, their places of worship, their communities.

Remember, breaking through the 600 MOC barrier immediately raises your influence and effectiveness and opens the door wide open for further growth, which we'll address in another book. We're talking about your personal power, or Influence Power™, not your positional power. If you're currently in a particular leadership role, you may have a certain amount of positional power (which is really force, not power). For example, a Father or Mother might have positional authority in the family. We're talking far beyond that.

Imagine that 80% of your current influence is due to your position. That's pretty typical. Now imagine holding the positional influence constant and raising your Personal Influence to the point it is now 90% of your total influence. Now you have some serious influence. That happens naturally with a major consciousness shift beyond the 600 MOC barrier.

At the same time your interests are shifting to what is best for all involved—Hey, I'm not suggesting you don't already think that way. :-)

More about how I'm coming up with these numbers later. It's another concept to be integrated, and it's an important one. It also was introduced to me through Dr. Hawkins and his mentors.

When you break through this glass ceiling, your natural Influence Power jumps dramatically—by orders of magnitude! Leadership is about influence. Your natural leadership ability jumps dramatically when you make this breakthrough.

This book is about how to break through the glass ceiling.

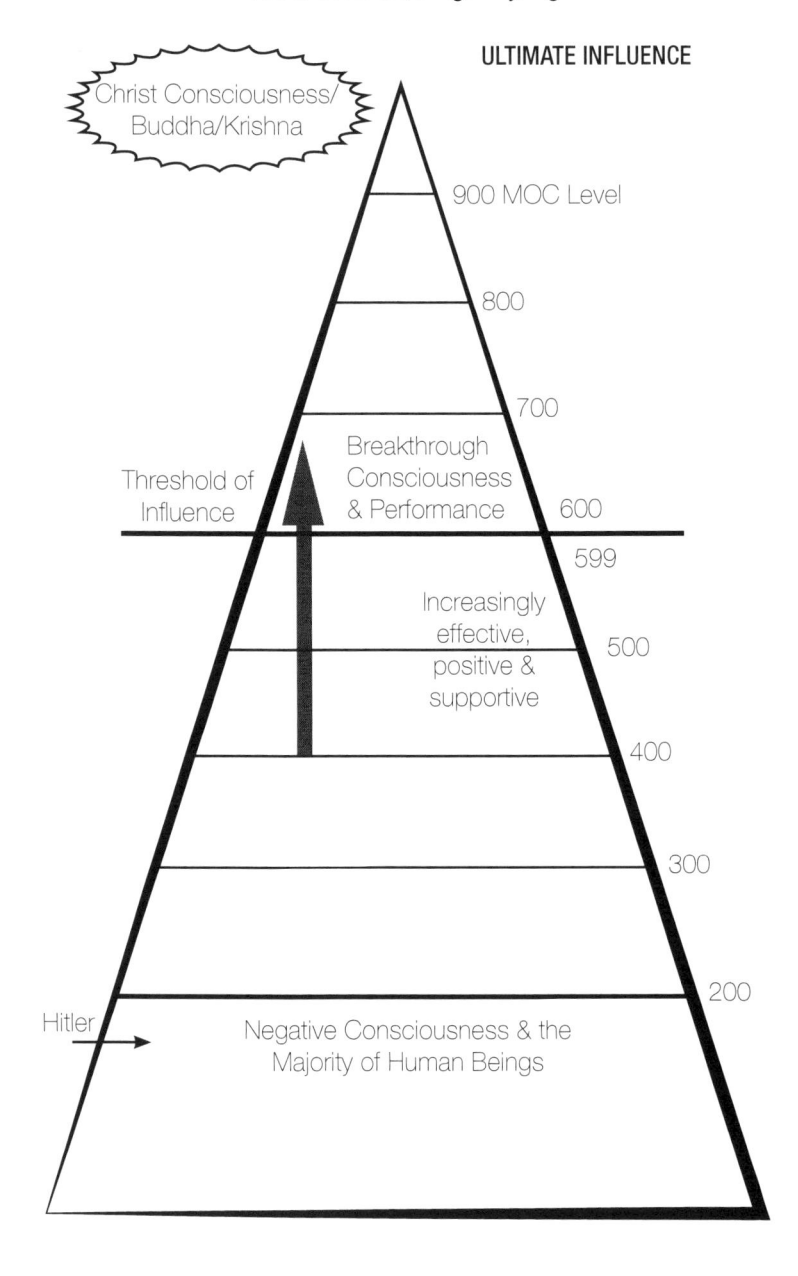

Shift Consciousness, Change Everything!

ULTIMATE INFLUENCE

Christ Consciousness/ Buddha/Krishna

900 MOC Level

800

700

Breakthrough Consciousness & Performance — 600

Threshold of Influence

599

Increasingly effective, positive & supportive — 500

400

300

200

Hitler →

Negative Consciousness & the Majority of Human Beings

Why Would I Want to Go to India?

Several years ago, on a whim, my wife and I went to a Oneness Movement conference in Denver and became Blessing Givers. This is a spiritual group, but definitely not religious. I've met people from numerous religions there.

We never used it much, mostly giving ourselves Blessings, or Deeksha. We have a number of friends in that movement, and it has a very important mission—to raise the consciousness on the planet as fast as possible. It's having some great success! The "tipping point" has been passed! It's about time, after decades of work by many people. People in other groups around the world have been working on the same mission in different ways. It's a very worthy mission.

The reason this is so important is that the behaviors of people follow their level of consciousness, as stated in Dr. Hawkin's subtitle: *The Hidden Determinants of Behavior*. It is for the benefit of us all to raise the consciousness, thus improve the behaviors of everyone on the planet.

During the last several years, a number of friends went off to India to the Oneness University. If it was possible to have "less than no" interest in going to India, that was me.

Friday, February 22nd, my wife was in Australia and I decided to attend the Oneness event at Evolve Expo in Denver that night. I was still struggling with the discomfort of a major rash, though significantly better now, and I thought some serious meditation might help. Two things happened that night:

- I had a 30 minute meditation experience in which I had absolutely zero pain or itching. I could have stayed in that space for hours. It was amazing.

- I heard my friend and prominent eye surgeon, Dr. Bill Hines, describe his trip to Oneness University in India and how his life would never be the same because of what happened to him in the process.

After the wonderful experience with the meditation, I talked with Bill about his experience and was impressed. I told him I wanted to go. "How about April 1st?" he asked. I pulled out my iPhone and asked him how long it was — thinking it was a few weeks long. "For you, only six days!" he said. "I'm in," I responded!

Why Would I Want to Go to India?

They had put together a special six-day program for business leaders, which was much, much shorter than their normal program. We can sponsor other business leaders like you to attend that as one of your options for breaking through the Threshold of Influence.

That gave me a little over a month to prepare. I work well under real deadlines, so I got a huge amount of work done. I also cranked up my health improvement program, knowing it would be painful on such long flights if much of my rash was still extensive.

It was an amazing month. I got a lot of work done, I accomplished some improvement in the rash, among other things now knowing what I could eat and what I could not, and I left for India to start class near Chennai on April 1st. The entire intent of the class was to "Awaken" the participants. I still wasn't quite sure what that meant, but it sounded encouraging—though I was uncomfortable with the term "Awaken" outside that close-knit community—even from the Founder of Enlightened Leadership! I'd have to find something better for the business community if I were ever to have reason to discuss it.

At Oneness University

We started class at 6:30am and went to 8 or 9pm. It was intense. There were educational sessions and experiential sessions. The educational sessions talked about expectations for Awakening and why it is important. I'm going to speak of this from the personal impact side here, then link it to leadership later.

They discussed a number of Liberations, i.e., issues from which we would be liberated once Awakened. Now it was getting interesting. Here are some of those areas:

Psychological Suffering—I'm not quite clear what that means, but my pendulum sure did. I'm pretty sure I was the only one there testing where I was on each and every area for which we could expect liberation. I set up a scale from 0 to 100%, where 0% would be ideal. A later chapter will explain how I did this.

I calibrated at 95% on psychological suffering. I was shocked. That's embarrassing! I checked a few people around me and then felt a little better. :-) Obviously, this is a big deal! Yes, I have found I can test other people without a problem. I do ask the pendulum, which is really asking my Higher Self, if its okay to do so.

Let's look at other "liberations." I won't try to explain them if I think they are clear. I'll get more descriptive on our website at some point. Be sure to register at http://www.enleadership.com/breakthrough/shift.

Fears—We only covered four of the most common fears in this class:

Fear of Failure

Fear of Rejection

Fear of the Future

Fear of Death.

I actually didn't do too badly here, averaging 20% across the four.

Mental Conflict—36%

Hurt—20%

Dissatisfaction—22%

Being Judgmental—26%

Having Attachments—32%

I was feeling pretty good at this point after the shock of 95% psychological suffering, but I should have held my celebration. :-)

Pleasure-seeking (in a way that consumes your effectiveness)—46%. Oops.

Day-dreaming (waste of energy)—25%

Here comes the killer for me. Really embarrassing!

Living Up to an Image—75%. Ouch!

Trying to Change Who We Are—56%

Worry—45%. Why did I learn this pendulum thing, anyway? No one around me had any numbers. They were safe and happy in their ignorance.

Mind Chatter—Oh yeah! 52%

By now, I'm really wanting to know what Liberation from all these looks like!

Boredom & Loneliness—7%. Much better!

Feeling Empty Inside—16%

Craving (a big step up from simple desire)—41%

Need for Permanence—36%

Seeking Perfection—6%. Aren't I good!

Living Outside of the Present (wasting energy, focus, etc.)—36%

Okay, now that you know I have flaws I didn't even know I had, are you still with me? Have I lost any respect I might have gained?

There were others, but I think you get the point.

Is This Religious?

One of the things that was very important to me was to see so clearly that the people at Oneness University were not trying to get anyone to worship some guru. It was not religious, either, as they had an alter with numerous icons to fit whatever religion you might come from. Buddha, Christ, Mother Mary, Krishna and many others I did not recognize were represented. The founders of the movement were there, too, and many people showed much gratitude for them. They are a couple, Sri Amma Bhagavan, and they have done a huge amount over the last several decades to further the cause of raising human consciousness—their clear purpose in life. They deserve much honoring and gratitude.

The movement does believe in the importance of you being clear about your own God, Divine, Higher Self—however you express it. If you have a Christian background and values as I do, your Divine would likely be Jesus Christ.

I gained perspectives I never had before about the miracles in my life that happen every day. By acknowledging and showing gratitude for these miracles, they are accelerating. My life is full of miracles. I am blessed beyond what I can express in writing at this time, but additional books will follow.

So, to be clear, raising your consciousness is a personal spiritual quest, available to individuals in any religion or non-religion, that will enhance your life in many ways.

Some Amazing Gifts I Received

The first time it happened was a couple days into the week. I went to bed beating myself up for feeling that I didn't have a very close relationship with "my Divine." This was based on our discussions that afternoon about the importance of having a personal relationship with your God, Higher Self, etc.

So, I set my iPhone for a 5:45am alarm and fell asleep while praying about it. Because I still had some rash, sleep was still not ideal. I would often wake up after only one dream cycle of sleep. That night, I gradually began to wake from a deep sleep realizing I needed to go to the bathroom. I guessed it was around 2 or 3am. I swiped my iPhone so I could see the time and discovered it was 5:42am. I had slept deeply all night and awakened naturally just before the alarm went off. That was a miracle!

I was giddy with joy. I giggled with laughter—joyful from my experience. And I immediately started profusely thanking my Divine. I couldn't stop laughing with joy. Then suddenly, I had a realization.

I already have a GREAT relationship with my Divine. Over the last year or so as I've been dealing with my healing process, I have been asking for help continuously of what I call my God Team, which includes Christ, my guides, my angels, my Higher Self, and a very special group, my Medical Assistance Program (MAP) Team, which also includes my Higher Self. See Appendix for reference to MAP Team, which comes from a book by Machaelle Small Wright, founder of Perelandra.

I just never used the "my Divine" terminology. This team has meant EVERYTHING to me over the last year. I have asked for help, gotten it, and shown lots of gratitude every miraculous little step of my healing process. This has all happened numerous times a day!

I was elated with the realization.

About that time, my iPhone buzzed a message, "Katherine Dedonis-Oakley has joined Viber." That's my younger daughter in San Diego. Another miracle because of the timing. Viber is an app that allows free phone calls or texts anywhere in the world.

I simply pressed CALL beside her name, and the next thing I know she was saying, "Hellooo?" totally surprised she'd get a call

Some Amazing Gifts I Received

right after downloading the app. The miracle of the timing allowed me to share the breakthrough I'd had overnight and the realization of the great personal relationship I have with my Divine. It was a blessing talking with her right then. It was great for our relationship.

Then I joyfully went off to class and shared my story with the group of 75 or so. At breakfast break, my new friend Todd came up to me and said, "From everything I'm experiencing with you this morning, I think you might be Awakened. Do you think you are?"

"I don't think so," I responded. The question was a shock. I never thought about it. I was just being me. I pulled out my pendulum and tested a couple of the Liberations, having no idea what to expect. Remember Psychological Suffering? It had gone to ZERO. From 95%, it had gone to zero. So had everything else I tested. Oh my, is this what Awakening is all about? I was elated!

It was a marvelous day. Highly energized. 100% focused on the instructors, feeling very connected with everyone. Awesome day. Because of the high energy of the day, I had a hard time getting to sleep that night. I woke up really grumpy the next morning! I struggled all day, finding myself judging the instructors, having a hard time staying awake in class, and on and on. So much for being Awakened. I clearly was not.

So, it turns out that I experienced an "awakened state," which is not permanent. It is also a peak energy situation that is not the same as a sustained, permanent Awakening.

But what a blessing for me as I went in and out of an awakened state several times that week. I got to fully experience "normal" life with all the conflict, hurt, living up to an image, psychological suffering and the contrast when I was completely liberated from all that.

When the permanent Awakening finally did happen on the last day of the class, I knew what to look for in understanding what was happening and integrating the experience as quickly as possible back into my real life. And it was NOT the peak, unsustainable situation of the awakened state. It is much more subtle. The changes have occurred, but it is not as obvious as a peak state. You learn how to integrate the changes in your life and get more and more value every day.

I also had a way to test if something had really happened—I could test to see if the issues of liberation had dropped from their peaks. So far, when it happened, everything went to zero. But I could not imagine maintaining zeroes in the real world. If possible, that certainly would be an ideal world. That would just have to be part of my research.

Breakthrough Research on the Flights Home

As I boarded the Lufthansa flight heading home, I was running on questions like, "What just happened to me?" and "How can it be explained more scientifically?" and "What do I already know that somehow ties to this?" and "How can I explain this to business associates without using this 'awakened' terminology?"

So once we were in the air, I turned on some soft music and lost myself in the quiet world of a noise-reduction headset. I pulled out my notebook dedicated to this project and started thinking.

While the Oneness instructors talked about raising consciousness on the planet, they never really tied "awakening" to consciousness. Is there a direct relationship?

I thought of Dr. Hawkin's Map of Consciousness. Problem is, I've never been able to measure MOC. I wonder if somehow because of what happened that I could now? Oneness Movement instructors said there was literally a neuro-biological change in our brains.

So, what the heck. I got to work to see if I could do this now. I had tried to test my MOC before and got huge numbers—like up close to the 1,000 of Christ Consciousness, so I had a pretty clear hint THAT was wrong.

Let's see what it says now. Hmmm. 615. Is that real? Not sure, but it sure seems more likely to be accurate than 900+! :-)

So, I thought, who else could I test? Of course! Other people in the Oneness Class who had "graduated" (The Oneness Movement now guarantees either Awakening while in India or your date of Awakening, usually soon thereafter).

I listed some people I had met. I tested the pendulum to see what I got for their MOC's. I was getting numbers like 612, 618, 621, 608. Very interesting. A clear trend, but how could I know what it meant?

I then asked, "Are these accurate?" and got a very clear YES! Cool! That's a first for MOC.

I needed comparisons. So, I thought of friends back home who I consider high consciousness, but they have not been through this program. I picked some of my wife's long-term meditation students and a few others back in Denver. I wrote down about ten of them who're definitely all highly conscious.

I started measuring the first person. 599. Interesting.

The second person: 599. Really!

The third person: Want to guess? You got it, 599.

All ten had an MOC of 599. These are people who had been part of meditation classes and other consciousness-raising approaches for quite a few years, and they're all sitting right at a breakthrough point in consciousness!

Do you see the accidental discovery? Awakening relates to a consciousness shift to an MOC of over 600!

I knew that the primary tool of Awakening for the Oneness Movement is the Deeksha, or Blessing. Deeksha is an ancient Sanskrit term for blessing or initiation. We'll use Blessing and Deeksha **interchangeably**.

So, I should be able to give Deeksha and raise people from 599 to above 600, right?

That brought up some more questions:

Has the effectiveness of my Deeksha improved since the Awakening process?

Remember, all pendulum work is done with statements, but I find it easier to talk about it with questions, so forgive me for doing that.

Questions:

Is my Blessing more powerful than a week ago? YES

If my old Blessing had a value of 100 on an infinite scale, what is the value/effectiveness/power of my "new" Blessing? 1 million

Wow, that's 10,000 times as powerful if I did the math right. No wonder the old Deeksha never seemed to do anything! Now, in this case, do I really care whether it is 7,000 or 15,000? Not really. I just wanted to know if it was a big number. I'm not apologizing for my precision, but it would be hard to validate the actual, precise number. Do you hear me covering my butt? :-)

Ah. Another question. Can I predict the number of my Blessings needed to take a person from 599 to over 600? YES

How many? 35. Interesting. That's a lot, but doable.

Does everyone who is at 599 need the same number? NO

Can I predict the number they need? YES

Ok, back to the high-consciousness Denver list. I started measuring the number of Blessings they needed from me to break through the 600 barrier.

24, 12, 15, 22... It varied quite a bit, but none over 35, and I realized I had an experimental laboratory waiting for me at home. These are all open-minded people. Some of them are even Oneness Movement Blessing Givers. Exciting!

So now, I don't need to talk to business people about Awakening, which technically I don't have the right to do from Oneness University anyway. Instead, I can discuss what happens when you breakthrough the 600 barrier on the Map of Consciousness scale. While that's still a little weird, it's much more comfortable to discuss. It doesn't have the same "charge" for me as "Awakening" does.

Back Home from My Transformational Experience

Back home, I found myself a little sluggish, which was suggested could happen as the new energies were integrating. I knew it wasn't jet lag, because that has never affected me much at all.

Being quick to measure, I thought I would track my progress. I brainstormed and measured the following factors from 0 to 100%, where 100% was back to normal:

	April 11
Motivation	68%
Energy	77%
Focus	70%
Clarity	72%
Creativity	76%
Embrace Life	83%
Clear Senses	81%
Awareness	82%
Functional	86%

Shift Consciousness, Change Everything!

Frankly, I was a little concerned as Oneness University talked about 6 weeks to 6 months to integrate. I wondered if my "effectiveness" would be lowered for a substantial time.

But look what happened over the next few days:

Dates:	11th	12th	13th	14th	16th	17th	21st
Motivation	68%	84%	95%	107%	114%	122%	128%
Energy	77%	88%	96%	100%	114%	120%	124%
Focus	70%	89%	96%	107%	112%	124%	128%
Clarity	72%	91%	95%	107%	112%	126%	130%
Creativity	76%	89%	97%	109%	114%	128%	132%
Embrace Life	83%	94%	99%	108%	113%	120%	126%
Clear Senses	81%	93%	97%	100%	105%	120%	124%
Awareness	82%	96%	98%	108%	115%	121%	126%
Functional	86%	97%	99%	100%	100%	100%	100%

Now, I'll bet I know what you're thinking. The same thing that I did when it first happened on April 14th. How could anything like Motivation be more than 100%?

After thinking about it and doing some testing, I realized it makes total sense. These measurements were set up as % of "normal." That was the old normal. It could very well be different now with the consciousness shift. And you know something? When my motivation was showing 128% on April 21st, I felt it! It was and still is real. Nothing has dropped off. And I suppose you cannot be more than 100% Functional. That's how I interpret that consistent number.

The Surprises Continue

Okay, next surprise. Look what happened on April 27th:

	April 27
Motivation	200%
Energy	200%
Focus	200%
Clarity	200%
Creativity	200%
Embrace Life	200%
Clear Senses	200%
Awareness	200%
Functional	200%

What? Everything solidly and exactly 200%? A huge and precise jump? Nothing at 195 or 210?

Why 200% and why now?

I was baffled.

But I trust the measurement. So nothing to do but look for what else has changed. Something significant? Hmmm. Consciousness maybe?

I turned to my Map of Consciousness measurements. Let's verify my MOC. I know I had an amazingly lucid and powerful dream last night, but did something else happen?

Wow! I don't know why, but my MOC level had jumped substantially. I cannot explain why, but what I've learned is that as soon as we free ourselves from the solid glass ceiling at 599 MOC, the Threshold of Influence, we're off and running on a whole new personal growth curve. We're free to grow again, no longer stuck. Small, continuous consciousness shifts become commonplace. These are all little miracles, as they are simply Divine Grace. And what keeps them happening is Deeksha and gratitude – and maybe other things I don't know about yet.

So my motivation, energy, focus, clarity, etc. had jumped dramatically with a jump in consciousness. Did I mention that there are a lot of benefits of continually developing your consciousness?

As I write this over a month later, I can tell you my motivation, clarity, focus, creativity, energy continue to be consistently at LEAST 200% of what they were a few months ago. I feel it every day. I'm stoked! I will probably say more in an update on the website or next version of the book.

The Perfect Test Labs

On that long flight home, I realized I had two test labs available to me that were perfect.

I had tested the high-consciousness group in Denver for MOC, as I mentioned, and each one I listed was at 599. Understanding what I know now, that doesn't surprise me. But what an opportunity to see if I can predictably get them above 600 MOC—above the glass ceiling.

Some of them were better friends of mine than others, and some also needed fewer Blessings, based on my pendulum, to breakthrough the 600 level MOC, so I selected four of those: Jim, Barbara, Ev and Aurelia. Arriving home, I knew I had about ten days before I was off to Greece to meet my wife and her group. That would be the second test lab.

I called each of them, described my experience in India, told them what I had learned on the flights back and invited them to participate in my experiment. They all readily agreed, and we started setting times for Deeksha. Two of them were already Blessing Givers through the Oneness Movement, which had the extra value that if they broke through the barrier, their Blessings or Deeksha would become many times more powerful. Exciting!

I started with Jim, who is currently living with us. This was especially good because he is so open to my sharing everything.

We talked about everything, then did some pre-testing on some elements that should be impacted by a breakthrough. Here, on a scale of 0-100%, is how he measured on some of the series of common issues we all have. We'll address these further in another chapter.

Psychological suffering	86%
Fear of rejection	87%
Fear of the future	42%
Fear of death	20%
Fear of failing	22%
Conflict in the mind	31%
Hurt	41%
Living up to an image (actually one of my big ones) :)	15%
Worry	41%
Need for permanence	35%
Living outside the present	75%

The Perfect Test Labs

These are very personal. Thank you so much, Jim, for letting me share them.

I already knew how many Deeksha I was projecting he needed, which was 15. He was open to having a lengthy session, so we discussed it and decided to give a very lengthy Blessing. I had tested that it was totally okay and safe to do so. One minute or less is a typical time.

So, on April 19th, I did a long Blessing, several minutes, and when finished, we talked about the experience. It was actually quite powerful for me—and never had been before my own shift. It was significant for Jim, as well. He knew something was happening.

I tested to see how many we had remaining to do: 9 remaining. Okay, good progress.

He was open, so we did another lengthy one. Afterwards, the measurement said we had 5 remaining.

I was excited, and so was Jim, so we decided to do one more that day, then continue the next day.

So, I did a nice long Blessing, probably 3-4 minutes. Toward the end of it, I suddenly felt a brief, sharp, clear buzz under my left hand, which was on his head. It startled me, and I opened my eyes for a moment to see what had happened. It lasted less than half a second, but was very interesting. I wondered if it signaled completion. I remember being told at Oneness University that there was actually a neuro-biological change that happens in the brain in the awakening process.

I immediately tested Jim for MOC and was actually a little surprised that it was still 599. Was I missing something? Were my theories not proving out in the lab?

I was eager to complete this, but I tested to see if it was okay to do more and got a firm NO. So I suggested he integrate what had happened and that we get together the next day. He agreed. We parted company.

Jim works in senior caregiving, so he later headed off to his overnight job.

An Amazing Experience

So, I was deeply sleeping that night when all of a sudden I got this voice so strong in my head that it woke me up. "Jim is awake and doesn't know it." I sat up in bed, first looking for who was in my room who said that. I switched on the bedside lamp, looked at the clock and it was exactly 3:00am. I always find it fascinating when things happen at such precise points.

I grabbed my lab notebook and my pendulum. I immediately measured Jim's MOC. It was 608, thus over the threshold of 600! Wow!

To test further, I tested each of the personal issues we had pretested.

- psychological suffering: Was 86%. Now 0%!
- fear of rejection: Was 87%. Now 0%!
- fear of the future: Was 42%. Now 0%!
- fear of death: Was 20%. Now 0%!
- fear of failing: Was 22%. Now 0%!
- conflict in the mind: Was 31%. Now 0%!

- hurt: Was 41%. Now 0%!
- living up to an image: Was 15%. Now 0%!
- worry: Was 41%. Now 0%!
- need for permanence: Was 35%. Now 0%!
- living outside the present: Was 75%. Now 0%!

He really has broken through the Threshold of Influence! My first lab success, and I'm so excited for Jim.

I know you're thinking, 0%? Is that really possible? We asked the same question for our own sake, as well as those with whom we're working. The research coming up shortly.

When Jim Came Home

I was waiting for him—sitting on the stairs in the foyer as he entered the front door. Jim had no clue what had happened, and here's why.

After the consciousness shift, Jim's brain was running on a new operating system. The new operating system doesn't know about the old one. It just knows how to operate now.

So, until Jim starts looking for differences, he literally won't realize there are differences. He just experiences what he experiences.

So, I started asking questions about how he felt, how that's different than when he normally finishes a nights work?

Also, other things, like "we've talked about the mind chatter" that's always going on in our mind. What's that like now? With these questions, Jim began to realize something had really changed.

We coach people over the months after a shift, because they do need to know what to look for. The one thing everyone seems to realize first is the calmness of their mind (the lack of so much mind chatter, or thought disturbance).

We were moving forward, and I felt good about our experiment.

Did Those Psychological Suffering and Other Numbers Stay at Zero?

Wouldn't it be nice if they did. What really happens is they slowly start coming back up until they settle into a new place. But the new place is very different.

Here are Jim's facts nearly a month later when things had smoothed out:

	Apr 19	Apr 20	May 16
Psychological suffering	86%	0%	16%
Fear of rejection	87%	0%	17%
Fear of the future	42%	0%	16%
Fear of death	20%	0%	6%
Fear of Failing	22%	0%	4%
Conflict in the mind	31%	0%	6%
Hurt	41%	0%	5%
Living up to an image	15%	0%	3%
Worry	41%	0%	9%
Need for permanence	35%	0%	8%
Living outside the present	75%	0%	30%

I think you'll agree that these are huge shifts—all created by a simple shift in consciousness. And Jim feels it. This book is about how to do that. But you have to see the value in even wanting it first!

What would be the value of just one of these shifts? If you could permanently remove 70% or more of the psychological suffering you're now enduring, what's the value of that alone? Of course, results vary. :-)

I wonder how much money in therapy fees it would take to get the same results? Or could you even get those results? :-) No offense to effective therapists. I'm actually a fan of Brief Therapy.

What About the Other Experimenters?

Before heading for Greece, I took our other three volunteers across the Threshold of Influence barrier to over 600 MOC. Two of them started giving high-powered Blessings and reported great results in terms of what they felt and what the receiver experienced.

Then twelve other experimenters joined us in Greece. While that's a lovely place to do this work, it would bore you to tears to look at each individual situation. I decided, instead, to share some data that shows the average value all of us received in the process. There are nineteen total people involved, including myself.

So, averaging everyone's pre- and post-breakthrough data, here is what we have. Note that there are two pieces of data:

1. The average of all nineteen people's initial numbers for nineteen different issues ex-

pected to be liberated by breaking through the 599 barrier.

2. When they shift, all the numbers go to zero. That will not hold up, unfortunately. After several weeks, the numbers for each person and each issue settle into a constant. It is this steady number that we are averaging for all participants to determine average end value. We've used the 30-day point, because everyone's numbers settled out by then. Note: Even though they are already excellent, we haven't given up on continuing to improve these numbers. It's part of ongoing research. Check the website to see the latest.

ISSUE	(19 people) Initial Average	30 days after breakthrough, settled into constant (average)
Psychological suffering	85%	26%
Average of four fears	25%	12%
Conflict	36%	18%
Hurt	42%	20%
Dissatisfaction	28%	13%
Being judgmental	26%	10%
Having attachments	39%	13%
Pleasure-seeking	37%	17%
Daydreaming	31%	10%
Living up to an image	75%	21%

What About the Other Experimenters?

Trying to change who we are	55%	15%
Worry	36%	17%
Mind chatter/thought disturbance	32%	12%
Boredom & loneliness	12%	6%
Feeling of emptiness inside	32%	15%
Craving	44%	16%
Need for permanence	36%	13%
Seeking perfection	51%	17%
Living outside of the present	76%	40%

Of course, no one is average. These numbers are hard data to give you some idea of average value of the shift to above 600 MOC. Your numbers would be higher for some things and lower for others.

Also, as we saw with Jim, when you continue to grow your consciousness, these numbers can drop even further at certain milestones. We're still trying to understand the significance of these milestones, as we saw the same phenomenon with the several people that have reached 660 MOC.

Just take one of these as an example. The average of nineteen people for "Living Up to an Image" was 75%. Ouch. Happens to be exactly my number. Imagine the psychological energy wasted in that effort. That's energy not available for focusing on your next business breakthrough. Now, feel that dropping to 21%. What a release of "opportunity energy." And that is just one element.

What would even these average post-shift numbers mean to you if you could have them?

Can you see how the release of all the wasted energy in dealing with all these issues is energy that you could use to be a much better leader?

Maybe an Even Bigger Factor

One more thing I haven't mentioned yet. There is a Forward Focus™ element we've also been tracking. For some people, this factor might mean more than all the others.

"Clarity of Who You Are" is the element. We haven't mentioned it because it is not an issue per se. But let's look at the average numbers pre- and post- breakthrough.

	Pre-breakthrough average	Post-breakthrough average
Clarity of Who You Are	24%	96%

Do you think this level of clarity about who you are might be useful to you?

How would it help you focus? By knowing who you are at such a high level, imagine how clear you would be about moving forward. And how you're not wasting energy trying to figure it out every day. You'd have a solid, guiding compass.

I see this as one of the most important gifts from the breakthrough.

Let's take this idea a little further. It's not just about having more clarity about who you really are, but the behavioral side. How you show up is very important. Remember, consciousness is the "hidden determinant of behavior." So, as your consciousness rises above the Threshold of Influence, you clear out more and more of the garbage of how you "think you should be or behave –" the learned behaviors. The real you starts emerging, and THAT is the very best you can possibly be! Furthermore, by definition, the more you are yourself, the more effective you are. As you become more and more of who you truly are, your influence begins to skyrocket.

Here are my own measurements for these factors. Remember, April 1st was just before my consciousness breakthrough:

	April 1	May 24
Being who I really am	48%	77%
Degree of personal influence	63%	85%

Whether you're leading, teaching, parenting or just being, the difference you'll make as your consciousness rises will become greater and greater.

Can you start to predict that some "leaders" you know might not be so high in the consciousness area?

A Breakthrough Realization

I woke up in the middle of the night in Crete with a thought. I had to test it. I hopped out of bed, grabbed my notebook and headed to another room where I could work without disturbing my wife.

I started writing down names of people who are clearly world-class influencers, not just highly successful people, but very influential on the world stage. I wrote down about a dozen of them, mostly people from the leadership development field with which I'm familiar. I'll only share a few here—from leadership and personal development experts to the Zappos founder, to just a couple of political figures (then we'll stay out of politics):

- Stephen Covey (both the late father and son)
- Tom Peters
- Ken Blanchard
- Marshall Goldsmith

- Jim Collins
- Wayne Dyer
- Deepak Chopra
- Tony Hseih (Zappos founder)
- Nelson Mandela
- Bill Clinton

I'm trying to stay with people that most everyone will know. I would love for you to nominate some women. I know some that fit, but I'm not clear everyone knows them. I've avoided the political arena, though there are some interesting ones. Margaret Wheatley is an example in the leadership development area.

I then tested their MOC numbers. The results did not surprise me. They were ALL over the 600 MOC Threshold of Influence—all 12 of the original world-class influencer list.

Then I created a list of highly successful people, many of them professional speakers, best-selling authors. Highly successful, but not yet world-class. Many of them friends. They were nearly all between 580 and 599 MOC—at a very high level of consciousness, but stuck under the glass ceiling. This did not surprise me either.

Let's be clear that there is a significant distinction in consciousness between those at 580-585 and those well above 590. Having said that, it is reasonably easy to get any

A Breakthrough Realization

of these people moving again—up the Map of Consciousness scale toward 599. They still have to know HOW to do that, but it's quite doable. The issue is the breakthrough to get above 600 from 599.

There were only a couple that were over 600 MOC. Those are likely world-class influencers, or on the way, and I wasn't clear about it.

So we have world class INFLUENCERS on the breakthrough side, and we have excellent, well-known experts on the other.

Then I asked a few additional questions:

Did world-class typically come before the consciousness shift? NO

Did the consciousness shift above the Threshold of Influence tend to occur before the world-class success? YES

What percentage of the world-class successes occurred AFTER the consciousness shift? 100%

Wow! What an opportunity there is for all the 599 level people who are already highly successful to shift consciousness and open up the possibility of World Class influence—which means they would be making an even bigger difference.

Remember, the scale is logarithmic! The change of Influence Power is a key element in leading to world-class success, and it escalates rapidly above the Threshold of Influence.

So, we "accidentally" discovered this Threshold of Influence™ beyond which your Influence Power™ jumps by orders of magnitude. That's right—orders of magnitude. When you speak or write from beyond this threshold, you're influencing people in magical ways, you're communicating at much deeper levels.

Now, be clear, the world-class influencers also were highly successful in their field of endeavor before breaking through that ceiling. Don't expect to have amazing Influence Power if you aren't already focused on who you are and what you're about. But if you're already making a big difference and you break through that Threshold of Influence, your Influence Power skyrockets.

So, how do you break through that glass ceiling? Soon.

I'm Supposed to Do What?

Once you've been blessed with the shift we're discussing, things happen rapidly. My daughter and I were taking a side trip to Santorini when I woke up at night AGAIN with a new, strong message, "You need to write a book about all this and do it quickly!"

Write a book? Okay, I've done that a few times. Write a book quickly? I've written several books, and I know what it takes. Quickly is not one of the parameters I've experienced.

But it was very clear, and remember, I'm super-motivated after the shift, so I immediately start taking notes in a special section of my notebook. And I know this is my Higher Self talking to me. It's been a great ride so far, so I'm listening!

Little did I know I WAS NOT going to write the book. My Divine, my Higher Self was going to write it. Virtually every day and night, I've had insights that had me writing, making notes or calculating data from all my records. Effortless work. Joyful work!

Then I talked to a bank teller and got great ideas on how the book should work. Almost every conversation I had about this topic gave me specific ideas.

I tested to determine it would be a short book, and even the ideal MOC level of the book to relate best to the right people. Remember, my testing is a connection to my Higher Self.

I've never had written pages flow through my fingers into the computer so easily. The ideas are there when I need them. I'm currently in the mountains to write, and here's how it's working:

- I'll wake up at various times of night inspired to write about a specific topic or idea. I'll whip it out very quickly. If it's nighttime, I'll go back to bed. When I wake up, more ideas are waiting.

- I get tired of writing for a bit, so I'll have a meal. As soon as the meal is over, here comes the flow of material again.

- Very little editing is needed, and I'm literally never stuck anywhere. If I get the least bit stuck, I'll take a break and watch some golf or send some emails. After a short break, the information is flowing again.

- When I don't feel like writing, I do some planning. Which chapters go where? What is the title of the book? What MOC for the book is best? What ideas have the best effectiveness quotient (this is a 0-100% test I set up to measure overall effectiveness, including the value to the reader, how it fits with everything else, it's importance in the overall scheme, etc).

- Several times when I've wanted a break, I've called a friend who knows what I'm doing. ALWAYS, I get fresh tweaks and ideas for the book.

I am wrapping up my fifth day, and the first draft of the book is finished. The piece I'm writing right now was an afterthought. The rest of the book is finished. My testing has told me where to slide this in.

Bottom-line, I've personally only written about 10% of this book. Guess what part that is—the part that is getting edited out. :-) The rest has been written through me by my Divine.

This has literally been the easiest project of this size I've ever done. Often, I run out of steam about 80% of the way through a project like this. Not so here. The energy, creativity and motivation have stayed constant throughout. What a joy!

Shift Consciousness, Change Everything!

Imagine your productivity and effectiveness in your leadership role having this super-productive mode. You will once you make your shift!

Oh, I Forgot to Wear My Reading Glasses

I had an experience today that is a great example of what happens in the shift process and you don't even realize it at first.

Over the last couple of months, my reading vision had gotten worse—to the point I needed to wear cheap, reading glasses. Over the last couple of weeks, I had surrendered to that need enough to start wearing the reading glasses on top of my head for ready access wherever I was. They are on my nightstand when I go to bed.

This morning I woke up with a few insights about the book, so I simply sat up in bed and grabbed my notebook, pen and pendulum.

I wrote about the insights, then turned to my "remote Deeksha list" (a list of people I'm doing the Blessings for everyday) and reviewed where people were. I'm either writing down tiny numbers reflecting their current MOC, or if they're at a boundary (499, 599), I'm writing the number of Deeksha they need to breakthrough the Threshold. To save space, I use a fine point pen and write very tiny numbers.

I did my remote Deeksha, took some additional notes, read through some notes from the night before and decided it was time for breakfast. As I turned to get out of bed, I noticed my reading glasses on the nightstand.

Wow! I had done all this work without a problem and never even realized I wasn't wearing the glasses. Now we can talk about the Divine gift, the miracle, but I want to concentrate on the fact that I didn't realize anything had changed. It was only when I saw the glasses that I realized the blessing I had received.

That is what it is like when you breakthrough the Threshold of Influence! You might not even notice the distinctions from the old you. You have to watch for them, and we'll help coach you on what to look for.

Well, you've waited long enough. How do you get started?

How Am I Doing All These "Tests?"

This has to be a question you've been wondering about.

The concept is muscle testing, or applied kinesiology, or behavioral kinesiology. While this might be challenging to some, we've actually been demonstrating the basics of this capability during our various Enlightened Leadership workshops and seminar for many years. It always tends to stun some of the people in the room.

This concept is discussed extensively in *Power vs Force*. Dr. Hawkins refers to the initial of work of Dr. George Goodheart, who pioneered the specialty. He also refers significantly to the work of Dr. John Diamond, MD, who refined the specialty into what he called behavioral kinesiology. Dr. Diamond published a book in 1979 called "Your Body Doesn't Lie," a significant perspective involved here. We'll abbreviate this powerful tool as BK for behavioral kinesiology.

See Appendix for contact and services of Dr. John Diamond, MD.

If you've been to a chiropractor, you might have experienced the idea of muscle testing, where you held out your arm or held up your hand. They might have pressed on your arm or tried to separate your closed fingers. The idea is simple and proven, yet not widely understood. The idea is that your body and muscles are closely aligned with your Higher Self or Universal Energy, where truth vs fiction is known.

Did you get the significance of that comment—having access to knowledge of truth vs fiction, yes vs no, true or false?

In our workshops, we use the arm test, which Dr. Hawkins recommends. We'll have a big, strong guy come to the front of the room, and have him hold out his arm parallel to the floor. We'll say "be strong" and press lightly on his arm. The arm won't move much because it is strong. It will be solid. A "true" indication. We'll then have him state his name and hold strong. The arm will be strong because he is truly the name he said.

Then, we'll have him say something obviously false, like "my name is Susan." His arm will be easy to press down as it is weak. A "false" indication. His statement was false. It always shocks the big, strong man when he cannot maintain his strength while "lying." That's pretty clear, so we go to the next level.

We'll have him turn around away from the class, and give silent instructions to the class to send him silent but negative thoughts. We'll test his arm while that's going on and it will be weak—no matter how hard he tries to be strong. We have him state what he experienced. He knew it was weak. This gives you some idea of the impact of negative consciousness. The good news is that we don't have to be at the mercy of negative thoughts, and we demonstrate that in the class, as well. We simply instruct him to think about some joyful, loving moments in his life. Then the projected negative thoughts do not make him weak.

Because I cannot push my own arm down, I have become very proficient at using a pendulum for the same purpose. The pendulum is used to test "yes" or "no" based on the direction it moves. The trick, or the breakthrough, you have to accomplish is not letting your conscious mind influence the outcome. That's not easy for everyone, which is why we offer some of our testing services. You're looking for answers from your unconscious mind, which is far more powerful than your conscious, programmable mind. Your unconscious mind is constantly connected to the Higher Consciousness. It's like having access to the universal data base of information.

For more information on this, see references in the Appendix. It's important in this work, but far beyond the scope of this book to teach you how to do it.

I think a few words about how I came to be proficient in using the pendulum effectively might be useful. The year 2012 was one of the toughest years of my life. Very early I acquired a massive rash all over my body, to which I've referred several times earlier in the book. The itching was so bad at times, I would break down in tears. I could hardly wear clothes at the worst times because of the sensitivity of my skin. Even bed sheets irritated my skin. I was sleeping typically 4 to 5 hours per night.

When numerous doctors couldn't figure out the cause and only wanted to deal with the symptoms—namely cortisone shots to relieve the symptoms, I somehow knew that would be a mistake. If I removed the symptoms, I'd never deal with the real issues. At 64 years old, I saw this as the biggest wake-up call I'd ever received. I somehow felt there were important lessons for me to learn—deep issues to clear, even though I had done different modalities of therapy and healing work for many years.

One of the most important healing processes I used was Dr. Ed Carlson's Core Health and Heart Forgiveness courses (see Appendix for information). You can do these as a self-study course, but ONLY if you become very good at BK (behavioral kinesiology). Otherwise, you need a facilitator who does the BK testing for you. While I had been dabbling with kinesiology for years, I got very, very serious about it at this time—using it every day numerous times—getting better and better all the time. I knew I had become very good with it when my highly intuitive wife, Jonette Crowley, came to me and asked me to do some tests for her with my pendulum. :-)

Note: I just talked to Dr. Carlson, and he told me that telephone sessions with a facilitator are quite effective. I didn't think of that, but it makes sense. See Appendix.

This kinesiology is amazing stuff and will challenge some people's minds for sure. You'll have to trust this is real, or ... put the book away until you see other indications around you that this technology is real. It has been in effective use for a number of decades. There are a number of 100-hour Applied Kinesiology certification courses available from Los Angeles to New York City, aimed at professional health care providers. They're using the technology to let the patient's body tell them what is needed. That's a big deal! I honor them and have no doubt that these professionals know far more about this than I do.

An invitation: I'm happy to have my work validated by a trained professional in AK or BK. There are only two requirements. Their Map

Of Consciousness level must be over 600, as I've discovered that is critical for some of these measurements. They also must be able to measure MOC for themselves and others. Consciousness alone might not be sufficient for that measurement.

Here's what you can count on. Like Dr. Diamond's work, our results are predictable, repeatable and universal. If I state a calibration or number determined by my pendulum, you can be assured that I have tested that number in at least two ways, and more if I see how to do it. I won't state a result if it is not consistently derived over and over again.

Also, if we're measuring 0-100%, I'm not overly concerned if I'm off by 1%. I'm more interested in comparing numbers and consistency.

My pendulum is almost always sharp and clear—except when I'M not sharp and clear. I've learned not to even try using it in those situations. Occasionally, something has caused the pendulum to give reverse indications. Actually, it's not the pendulum, it's my issue when that happens. I've learned how to clear myself in those instances. It takes about 30 minutes before I'm ready to use the pendulum again. Or if I'm tired, I just might need to rest. If I do any testing in this environment, I come back and retest when I'm refreshed.

I hope this has been helpful to divulge. Again, I'm open to validation support! I'm quite comfortable with everything we're sharing here.

So, if I say something or someone calibrated at a certain level, I determined that from the pendulum. Using the pendulum, I might say, "This person calibrates at an MOC level 460 or greater and get "yes." Then 461 or greater and get "yes." Then 462 or greater and get "no." Then the number is 461. I'll then reconfirm that by saying, "This person calibrates at exactly 461." If I get a "yes," then I know the number. If there is any question about the clarity, I'll retest.

So, David Hawkins did it all with arm testing and we do almost all of it with a pendulum.

Frankly, it took over a year of practicing to get to the point of high confidence with the pendulum, which is to say, confidence that I am NOT influencing it because of what I want it to say. One of the greatest values I've found with the BK testing is when the answers are not what I thought they would be. That forces me to rethink the situation, and confirms that I'm not influencing the outcome.

My Ultimate Test of the Pendulum

I had kind of an "ultimate test" of my confidence in the pendulum recently when we were on the trip to Greece previously mentioned. I was asked to video a discussion, and I was setting up the tripod to do that. I was untangling the wired lapel microphone when I heard a noise like metal on rocks. I looked around and didn't see anything on the ground. Then I realized the clip for the lapel microphone was missing. That's what I heard, I thought. I was convinced of it. Several of us looked all over the ground for it to no avail. Someone suggested I ask my pendulum. Oh no! Something that can be completely verified right or wrong! Did I have the faith?

    I really had no choice. So, I asked if the clip was on the ground in this area. Actually, I make statements: The clip is on the ground in this area. NO. Scary, because I was convinced I heard it fall on the rocks.

It is on the trail between here and half way to the bus. NO. It is somewhere from the bus to half way down the trail. YES. It is on that part of the trail. NO. It is on the bus. YES. So, where on the bus would it be, I wondered? That's a big bus. Oh, maybe… It is in my backpack. YES.

I was nervous. But I felt I had to tell the truth, so I told a person near me that the pendulum said it was in my backpack on the bus. There! I had said it. So, I went back to the bus, grabbed my pack and started looking. Not finding it. Uh oh…

Wait! Here it is. It was in the backpack—just like the pendulum told me. That was a significant breakthrough in my faith in my ability to get out of the way and let the pendulum tell the truth.

How would the pendulum, muscle testing, AK, BK know that, you're wondering. Just imagine having access to the ultimate universal data base.

One more thing about this. Just because you can effectively use a device or technique to test does not mean you can automatically measure everything. One thing I've discovered is that the higher my consciousness is the more I can measure.

Truthfully, I tried for years to measure my and other people's MOC. The numbers didn't make sense. I was getting MOC for people that was so high they couldn't possibly still be on the planet. One thing I've learned to ask, "Is this accurate?" Sometimes it says no. I always chuckle when that happens.

I have found the biggest two factors determining accuracy or validity of the test is whether my consciousness is high enough to make that test and the quality of the question I am asking. The pendulum is pretty good at letting me know when the answers I'm getting might be invalid. So, I always ask questions like:

- this answer is valid.
- this answer is 100% accurate.
- I have the ability to make this measurement.
- I have permission to ask this question.

So, How Do You Break Through the Threshold of Influence?

I'm going to discuss four ways, but only three of them are choices.

Option A. Surrender and Ask for Help From God in a Difficult Situation

The first one is not a choice. It is circumstantial. It always relates to surrender to God, your Higher Self, your Divine (or whoever you honor in that role) in a difficult situation. Here are two examples:

For twenty years, Lyndon Johnson, in various positions of power in Washington, had aggressively fought any attempt to provide equal rights for blacks. He was a known leader in those fights.

On the day President Kennedy was assassinated and the Vice President became

President Lyndon Johnson, my tests show that he experienced a shift to over 600 MOC. While I cannot prove it, I believe Lyndon Baines Johnson, suddenly shouldered with the world's most powerful position, surrendered in prayer and asked God for help.

The first hint was his extraordinarily humane insistence that Air Force One would not leave for Washington until Mrs. Kennedy was on board, even though he knew she would not leave without her husband's body. So President Johnson, against strong advice would not let the aircraft leave until both Kennedy's were on board, which was hours later.

A bigger indication of a consciousness shift occurred a few months later when, against the strong recommendation of his advisors, and a 180 degree turnaround on his part, he introduced the Bill for the Equal Rights Amendment. His advisors said it was political suicide, and he simply said, "It is time."

Not known as an orator, quite the opposite, President Johnson then proceeded to introduce the Bill with a very impressive and persuasive speech that went far in influencing Congress to pass the Bill. His influence had jumped dramatically.

An example I witnessed myself happened recently when dozens of us were hiking up steep terrain to get to a famous cave in Crete.

So, How Do You Break Through the Threshold of Influence?

One of our group was a bit overweight and not in shape for such a hike. Immediately, she was far behind the rest of the group, having to stop often. I really didn't think she had a prayer of a chance to make it (no pun intended).

We were having lunch near the cave when this woman came walking up to the group, red-faced, crying—yet with a radiance about her. I sensed she had had a profound experience, and I knew what her MOC had been—below 600. I pulled out my pendulum and quickly determined she had made the leap beyond 600. I confirmed the next day that she had given up, surrendered, and asked God for help. In that moment, she had been given Divine Grace, which is what happens in this shift above the Threshold of Influence.

So, while these are great stories, and I've seen many others, you cannot plan those. You probably don't want to plan a major struggle so you to have a breakthrough in consciousness.

Option B. Utilize Your Local Oneness Movement Opportunities

If you live in a reasonably populous area anywhere in the world, you might very well discover a group of Awakened Blessing Givers (their terminology) in a local Oneness Movement group. Google them locally or go to the international website, www.OnenessUniversity.org. You'll find a lot of information there.

Getting Deeksha will raise your consciousness. Key here is getting the Blessings from those known to have met the Oneness Movement's criteria for "Awakened," because Deeksha from those people are far more powerful. This might be controversial, but all my tests show dramatic, consistent differences.

Their meetings are usually very inexpensive, often occurring at someone's home. If you see an ad for a number of Awakened Blessing Givers coming to a big event, consider going and going early. Often, they will be giving Blessings in a separate area before the formal meeting begins. My limited experience suggests that these people are likely Awakened Blessing Givers. This way, you could potentially get 3-5 powerful Deeksha at one event.

It occurs to me that there is another excellent sub-option here. By going to some of these meetings, you could look for an Awak-

So, How Do You Break Through the Threshold of Influence?

ened Blessing Giver who would like to work with you one-on-one. Not a bad option!

The only issue is you don't have a way of knowing where you are in your process. They cannot tell you your Map of Consciousness number or how many Blessings you need for a breakthrough. And they cannot currently tell you if you're Awakened (their terminology). You have to go to India for that.

Option C. Business Leaders Can Attend a VIP Six-Day Course in India

This is what I did, and it is very powerful and quick, as they guarantee you'll be Awakened (their term) while there, or you will receive a specific date of Awakening soon thereafter. I can assure you that means you've broken through the top level Threshold of Influence and will gain all the benefits we've been discussing.

This has the advantage of being quick. You'll also get a thorough education about the process, what to expect, their 21 Liberations, etc. It's a powerful experience, and you'll meet some terrific people.

If there is a downside, it is the expense. As well as the 7-9 days away from home and office, it will cost you from $8,000 to $10,000, depending upon cost of air travel, hotel selection going and returning, etc.

It is a very, very good solution if it fits your needs. We'll be happy to sponsor you if you fit the guidelines for being a business leader.

Option D. Utilize Enlightened Leadership's Accelerated Consciousness Program™

You can achieve the breakthrough to above 600 MOC and all the associated benefits without ever leaving home. We have proven the ability to accomplish the breakthrough by working with you completely remotely. If you're close by, it's nice to do some of it face-to-face.

The following activities would be involved in your personal breakthrough process:

1. We calculate the number of Blessings needed to achieve the breakthrough, as well as where you stand with the series of issues we've been discussing.

2. We begin daily remote Deeksha/Blessings to address to get you close to the breakthrough point. This could take one to three weeks. Remember, all the real value is coming to you as Divine Grace. As Blessing Givers, we're just facilitating the process.

3. We hold conference calls to answer questions and coach you about what is to come.

4. We update you weekly, or more often if you're close to a shift, about remaining Deeksha needed. These estimates are not always 100% accurate, but are always very close. It's not perfect, because the variable

length of our Deeksha means variable results.

5. When you are very close to breakthrough, we stop doing remote Blessings and schedule a specific time—usually 15 minutes—to work directly with you to facilitate the shift. We do this so you are conscious of what is happening. It helps raise your awareness of the actual experience of breaking through the glass ceiling.

6. Once the shift has occurred, we coach you through periodic conference calls to help you fully and effectively integrate what has happened into your daily life. We can arrange for this to be private discussions if important to you.

7. You'll also have two private 60+ minute coaching calls to clear key emotions that will free you to continue your growth to the 700 level of consciousness and beyond.

8. We also coach you about integrating what is happening into your business if you have questions of this nature. This is about optimizing your leadership, formal or informal.

9. We start back daily Deeksha after the breakthrough to help you solidify and continue to raise your consciousness. We want you to go far beyond your initial breakthrough. We'd like to get you to the 660 MOC level, because there are some special things that

happen at that level. We'll discuss that in the next book.

10. Approximately one month after your personal shift, we recalculate where you are with the series of emotional/psychological issues and compare them to where you started.

11. We stay with you as coaches after your consciousness breakthrough long enough to get you to 699 MOC level.

NOTE: We do not have the authority from Oneness University to declare you "Awakened", as that's their term, and they only do that in India. We will focus completely on your MOC numbers, your percentage shifts from the issues from which you'll be liberated, your % increases in motivation, energy, focus, clarity, etc., and, of course, your experiences.

Brief Review of Options for Breaking Through the Threshold of Influence.

So, to review the options for your personal breakthrough:

A. Not a choosable option. It just sometimes happens.

B. Utilize Your Local Oneness Movement Opportunities

- very inexpensive if you have it locally
- value of getting involved with the group, regardless of how you accomplish the breakthrough
- no measurements available

C. Business Leaders Can Attend a VIP Six-Day Course in India

- guaranteed results for an investment of $8,000 to $10,000
- over and done in six days plus travel on each end

D. Utilize Enlightened Leadership's Accelerated Consciousness Program™

- guaranteed breakthrough to above 600 MOC
- you get to stay home
- we coach you before and after the process

- we'll stay with you to 699 MOC without additional charge
- reasonable fees

More important than which approach you choose is to make a choice. Raising your consciousness is critical to optimizing your effectiveness personally and professionally, and all your relationships.

After 25 years, Enlightened Leadership is excited to directly impact the consciousness and influence of people wherever they are and whatever their roles. It is time!

What's All This Got to Do With Transforming Your Life?

You mean other than everything? Let's just review ten of the factors that get liberated when we break through the Threshold of Influence:

Psychological Suffering

- average pre-shift is 85%
- average post-shift is 26%

To a significant extent, psychological suffering is a conglomeration of many mental/psychological issues that face us every day, including those we'll be discussing below and hurt, dissatisfaction, pleasure-seeking, mind chatter and craving. Because so many mental issues are involved, it's a big number—average 85% pre-shift.

This constant mish-mash of thoughts, judgments and questions fills our mind to overload, and that's the suffering.

When you break through the glass ceiling at the Threshold of Influence, this suffering drops dramatically. As you see, the average post-shift amount of psychological suffering is only 26% for our 19 experimenters who made the breakthrough. That's a huge difference. Imagine the freedom your mind would get to do conscious, focused, creative work—or play. You will have made room for so much opportunity.

Correction on that last comment. Through Divine Grace, you will have a mind with much room for focused, opportunity thinking. You cannot get this shift through psychological processes. You cannot will it upon yourself. It can only be achieved as a gift from your Divine, your Higher Self.

The majority of the struggle disappears, and you are blessed with a quiet mind ready for creating magnificence—at the same time your Influence Power skyrockets.

Fear of Failure

- average pre-shift is 27%
- average post-shift is 11%

Fear of the Future

- average pre-shift is 28%
- average post-shift is 12%

Let's deal with Fear of Failure and Fear of Future together. From an influence perspective, they are much the same, but they are somewhat additive. When you're feeling fear about an important situation in your life, you're also concerned about the future. When these fears are present in significant amounts (like 27% and 28%), the people around you feel your fear. That brings out their fear and stifles their creativity, problem-solving capability and invalidates the "shared" vision for the outcomes. This can quickly become a downward spiral.

The best thing you can do is eliminate the majority of your fears, and the Divine Grace that gets you above 600 MOC is how you achieve that. Once you're above the threshold, your continuing consciousness growth will lower the fears even more.

Conflict

- average pre-shift is 36%
- average post-shift is 18%

The myriad of conflicts we have going on in our minds is a big issue for all of us. We can easily become overwhelmed with:

- which is the best approach to solve this?
- can this person accomplish this job?
- how will I deal with this specific issue?
- how can I really decide priorities when everything seems important and urgent?
- how can I find time to deal with this family issue?

- how do I deal with this cash flow issue?
- and on and on. You know what I mean. You experience it every day (and night)!

Once you break through the Threshold of Influence, your issues don't disappear, but your mind is clear and only what needs addressing NOW shows up. You're not bombarded with everything at once. This is transformation in how you see the situation and your clarity in dealing with it.

Furthermore, my experience is that time actually seems to slow down. I used to look at the clock and be shocked at how late it was. I now find myself looking at the clock and being amazed at how early it is and how much I've already accomplished. it is quite freeing when so much more of your mind is suddenly available for creative use.

Being Judgmental

- average pre-shift is 26%
- average post-shift is 10%

While on the average, being judgmental is not as big an issue as some others, its really important because of the impact it has on those around you.

No matter what you say, if you are being judgmental about someone, they feel it, and it impacts their effectiveness. The feeling of judgment puts them in a funk, causes conflict and psychological suffering in their mind, even fear of the future, and their effectiveness and productivity fall accordingly. Your relationship is also compromised.

You know what happens next? Because they're even less effective, they feel more judgment from you, and a vicious cycle, a downward spiral is started. This is a lose-lose situation. This is great example of poor influence in action. I've sure been there—on both sides!

Substantially removing your tendency to be judgmental changes everything. After your shift, you'll still have judgmental thoughts, but very quickly you'll reflect on the situation, see the bigger picture better than ever before, and let go the judgment. It' amazing how people will respond differently.

Living Up to an Image

- average pre-shift is 75%
- average post-shift is 21%

You may or may not realize how much you're doing this, and of course, you're not average. Having said that, if the pre-breakthrough average over the 19 high-consciousness experimenters (Remember, they were all at 599) is 75%, there's a high probability this number is significant for you.

First, it's a huge waste of our energy. We have this image of the perfect kind of person in our mind, and we're constantly trying to be that person, show up as that person. By definition, that means we're not being ourselves.

Do you think people notice? You bet they do. They notice every little thing we do to show up like our ideal image. Because this happens a lot, they don't even know who we really are. It's hard to respect someone that we don't even know.

The irony is that the best we can be is who we truly are. The real "us" is special, and we don't see it. It's a trick of the ego mind that keeps us under control.

When the breakthrough occurs, there is a dramatic drop in our desire to be someone else. It opens up the real us, and people begin to understand who we really are. And you know what? They'll like what they see, and they know what to expect. They respond accordingly.

It was a huge shock to me as CEO of Enlightened Leadership years ago when my then COO had a heart to heart talk with me in which he informed me that he and everyone else in the company had a problem. They never knew which of the Ed Oakley's was going to show up for work. Ouch! Hope you cannot relate. :-)

Trying to Change Who We Are

- average pre-shift is 55%
- average post-shift is 15%

What's All This Got to Do With Transforming Your Life?

I probably could have combined this one with Living Up to an Image. The fact that the average of our experimenters (and they're pretty successful people) calibrated at 55% for Trying to Change Who We Are suggests that many people don't tend to like their perception of who they are now.

They wouldn't be trying to change if they liked who they saw in the mirror. Again, if you feel it, everyone who looks to you for leadership will feel a bit of it, too. Then they'll hold back just a bit on things like commitment to you and your mission.

The average shift is from 55% to 15% after the breakthrough. That's pretty dramatic, and you'll be thanking your Divine for the gift of Grace.

Worry

- average pre-shift is 36%, but much higher for some.
- average post-shift is 17%

You've probably heard the saying, "Worry is a prayer for what you don't want." There is a lot of truth in that. When you're worried, that's where your focus is, and you get more of what you focus on.

Furthermore, all the brainpower you use in worrying is not available for finding solutions.

But it's not your fault. It's a natural part of the human condition—until you break through to the whole new consciousness curve above the Threshold of Influence. Your worry will drop off in a major way. The way it still shows up is that a worry might enter your mind. Very quickly, though, you'll process that worry in a way you've never been able to at the lower consciousness level. Then it's gone.

What replaces it? Breakthrough solutions, ideas, clarity about what really matters.

Living Outside the Present

- average pre-shift is 76%
- average post-shift is 40%

We're not talking about when you are in an envisioning exercise. We're talking about our strong tendency (look at the pre-shift average) to spend a lot of our time thinking about:

- what might be
- what could be
- what it would be like if things were different
- what if we had a better partner
- what if we fired so and so
- what if we won that new client
- what if we had done that differently
- and on and on

I think you realize the issue. All the energy spent thinking about the future or the past is energy not available for dealing with what is happening right now.

Based on our experimenter's average post-shift number of 40%, it is not completely resolved by your breakthrough, but a lot of it is. Again these are averages. Your numbers may vary. :-)

Knowing Who You Are

- average pre-shift is 24%
- average post-shift is 96%

We've saved this one for last for several reasons. The average of our high-consciousness experimenters for Knowing Who They Are was only 24% before their shift. That included me, and that's scary low. If we don't know deeply and clearly who we are, no wonder we look to others to supply us an image to copy, an image to live up to.

If we don't know who we are, how can we expect others to know who we are? How can we trust ourselves? How can we expect others to trust us when they don't know who we are?

When we don't know who we are, we spend a lot of time and energy trying to figure it out.

Maybe something like this is how we got confused:

We were born perfect—in the image of God, if you will. Then things started happening that didn't seem to fit this perfection concept. For me, my Mom died when I was two years old, so I probably thought something must be wrong with me and filed away some false beliefs. Or maybe I even somehow thought it was somehow my fault. Ouch. That should make for some great beliefs about myself. :-)

Okay, this is a little heavy, but the point is that we start making little decisions about how things are and who we are. We start piling on these little limiting decisions, and first thing you know, we've confused everything and no longer know the perfection we were when we were born.

With the many layers of decisions and false beliefs, we've forgotten who we are and now spend a huge amount of energy trying to manage all these decisions and beliefs.

Good news!

Magic happens when we know who we are. It's never scary. Who we are is ALWAYS special and unique—certainly at the levels of consciousness for which this book was written.

When we know who we really are, we like what we see. We no longer have a reason to want to change ourselves. We no longer need to create a false image to live up to. We're totally okay just as we are.

Can you feel the energy we save by just being us?

Now, keep in mind that when you shift to above 600 Map of Consciousness level, you clear an amazing amount of the layers and layers of B.S.(can I say that?) we've built up over the years. We are stripped back to a clarity of not only who we are, but the specialness of who we are.

We have very exciting statistics for our 19 experimenters. After their gift of Divine Grace which led to jumping beyond the Threshold of Influence, on the average they went to 96% clarity in Knowing Who They Are. That's astounding!

And you know something? When they discovered at such a high degree Who They Really Are, they LIKED what they saw.

See, the REAL us is very, very special and indeed made in the image of God. Yet, in this breakthrough process, guess what is absent? EGO.

We feel good about who we are, but not in an egotistical way. We are comfortable in our own skin, and other people feel that. Then they feel comfortable around us. We are confident, but not egotistical.

My wife continues to tell me how much she appreciates and loves the person I've become. The irony? Me and everyone else who experiences this breakthrough in consciousness is simply returning to who they really were in the first place.

Don't put off returning to the specialness of who you are and becoming the best leader you can be. Choose an approach and go for the shift, the breakthrough, the return to clarity about Who You Are.

Then enjoy the dramatic increase in your Influence Power at the same time you're finding new ways to contribute to the health and welfare of your surroundings in a bigger way through your natural leadership.

IMPORTANT: When you make this consciousness shift above the Threshold of Influence, you haven't completed a goal as much as you've started a whole new growth curve. It puts you on a path to an enlightened way of being. Enjoy the journey and let us know how we can help.

LAST MINUTE COMMENT:

It is June 5th as I write this last edit. Something very interesting is going on that I cannot explain. There have been substantial upward consciousness shifts the last several days, and I don't know why. It happened May 31, June 1, June 4 and then TWICE during the early morning hours of Jun 5th.

Everyone we know who was already over 600 MOC got substantial increases in consciousness for each of those shifts, often putting them into the realm of entirely new capabilities. Those will be the subject of the Part 3 book.

Here's the surprise. NO ONE below 600 was affected. They got no value that we can tell. It almost seems like the HAVES and HAVE NOTS. I don't understand it, but it happened five times in six days.

Get yourself above 600 as fast as possible. Don't miss out on additional shifts that could come.

May your consciousness be your best friend.
:-)

APPENDIX

Dr. David Hawkins, MD, Ph.D

"Power vs Force: The Hidden Determinants of Human Behavior," David R. Hawkins, MD, Ph.D., Hay House, 2002

The author's publishing company has various interesting resources

Go to www.veritaspub.com.

"We can measure MOC for you if you like."

Contact Enlightened Leadership Solutions, Inc. if you'd like us to test your Map of Consciousness level. $25, which is applicable to services later if you choose to work with us. Call 1-303-729-0540. We will normally get this back to you within three days.

Get the latest updates and perspectives

Go to:
http://www.enleadership.com/breakthrough/shift/

Dr. John Diamond, MD

http://www.drjohndiamond.com, Dr. Diamond's website.

His book is "Your Body Doesn't Lie: Unlock the power of your natural energy." Looks like there's much more than muscle testing there.

Additional muscle testing or kinesiology:

The Perelandra organization, founded by Machaelle Wright, has some resources that will help some people learn to muscle test yourself—without the pendulum. It doesn't work for me, but I'm confident it does for many. Maybe I should try again, as there are definitely advantages of being able to muscle test yourself without having to have a pendulum handy. AND, if you can test via your fingers, you could do that under the table in a meeting. :-)

Description of Perelandra Kinesiology Testing Technique (Self-Testing)

http://www.perelandra-ltd.com/PKTT-Self-Testing-Steps-W75.aspx

There is also a video version on YouTube:

http://www.youtube.com/watch?v=oQXVTHvKNg&list=UUEUBEJMvZzlSwf4InTVf7KA&index=6

Using a Pendulum for Kinesiology

The best YouTube video I've been able to find on this topic is by Jonathan Livingstone.

He is a therapist who wrote the book, "The Therapist Within You: A Handbook of Kinesiology Self-Therapy with the Pendulum." The title of the book suggests you're finding your own answers.

I just bought the Kindle version of the book, but haven't read it yet. When I do, I'll update information on our website.

Here is the YouTube video where he shows how to use a pendulum:

https://www.youtube.com/watch?NR=1&feature=endscreen&v=-SS0C3lj3qs

A few comments I'd make. I grip my pendulum just about 3 inches from the weight so it doesn't take so long to "make up it's mind." :-) I cannot remember, but maybe I started out longer and tightened up the length as I became confident in how the pendulum was responding. I think he's pretty clear, but its important to realize that you need to discover what is "yes" and what is "no" for you and your pendulum. There are different ways they respond for different people. The key is to learn "together" what works for you. For example, my "yes" is an angle to the left between forward-backward and left-right. "No" is an angle to the right between forward-backward and left-right. You just have to figure it out by making statements where you KNOW the answer is yes, or no, and see what the pendulum does.

Core Health & Heart Forgiveness — Dr. Ed Carlson

Core Health & Heart Forgiveness are courses that are quite effective in eliminating limiting beliefs and healing old wounds. They have weekend courses that you can to physically go to, which has the advantage that they supply the people who can do the kinesiology/muscle testing for you.

Schedule of Courses Here:

http://corehealth.us/resources/events/

What I did required solid ability to do my own muscle testing. If you can do that, these are excellent self study courses. And now I've discovered they have facilitators who can do the testing for you over the phone!

Go to: http://corehealth.us/resources/

I personally did the Heart Forgiveness course and both Core Health Series I and II. It was a huge benefit to me in my healing. These courses include workbooks that give great explanation of the issues and solutions, as well as a workbook section. CDs are included that are used to process your issues. They are excellent.

My MAP Team

Machaelle Wright, Founder of Perelandra, also wrote a book that has been quite meaningful to me:

"MAP: The Co-Creative White Brotherhood Medical Assistance Program" (White here refers to a spiritual group representing all colors of the rainbow, thus "white.")

The book is available at:

http://www.perelandra-ltd.com or Amazon.com.

This has been very helpful in dealing with my rash over the last year plus. My MAP Team has been invaluable in solving problems for me of many kinds. It's a key way I established such a strong relationship with my Higher Self, my Divine.

Index

A

Accelerated Consciousness Program™, 93, 96
Awakened Blessing Givers, 90
Awakening, 29, 37, 38, 39, 40, 41, 43, 52, 92

B

Being judgmental, 30, 60, 102
Blessing, 25, 41, 42, 49, 50, 51, 59, 73, 74, 90, 91, 93, 94

C

Conflict, 101
Conflict in the mind, 50, 53, 57

D

Daydreaming, 60
Deeksha, 25, 41, 42, 48, 50, 51, 73, 74, 90, 93, 94
Diamond, Dr. John, MD, 75, 114
Dissatisfaction, 30, 60, 99

E

Enlightened Leadership, 93, 96, 97, 104, 113
Evolve Expo, 26

F

Fear, 30, 50, 53, 57, 60, 100, 101, 103
Fear of death, 30, 50, 53, 57
Fear of failing, 50, 53, 57
Fear of the future, 30, 50, 57, 100, 103

G

Goodheart, Dr. George, 75

H

Having attachments, 30, 60
Hawkins, Dr. David, MD, 19, 20, 113
Hurt, 30, 38, 50, 54, 57, 60, 99

I

Influence Power, 20, 22, 23, 67, 100, 110

K

Kinesiology, 75, 79, 114, 115, 116

Knowing who you are, 63, 107

L

Living outside the present, 50, 54, 57, 106

Living up to an image, 31, 38, 50, 54, 57, 60, 61, 103, 105

M

Map of Consciousness, 18, 21, 39, 43, 48, 67, 79, 91, 109, 113

Map of Consciousness level, 79, 109, 113

Mind chatter, 31, 55, 56, 61, 99

Muscle testing, 114

N

Need for permanence, 31, 50, 54, 57, 61

O

Oneness Movement Blessing Givers, 43, 50, 90

Oneness University, 26, 29, 33, 43, 46, 52, 95

P

Pendulum, 29, 30, 31, 37, 41, 49, 53, 73, 77, 78, 79, 80, 81, 83, 84, 89, 114, 115

Perelandra, 36, 114, 117

Pleasure-seeking, 31, 60, 99

Power vs Force, 19, 75, 113

Psychological suffering, 29, 30, 37, 38, 50, 53, 57, 58, 60, 99, 100, 103

T

Thought disturbance, 56, 61

Trying to change who we are, 31, 61, 104, 105

W

Worry, 31, 50, 54, 57, 61, 105, 106

Y

Your Body Doesn't Lie, 75, 114

About the Author

For thirty years, Ed Oakley has been on a mission to better understand human behavior and how to influence it. It started with two needs:

To better understand and improve his own behaviors. Really, how to bring out his best, which sometimes was difficult.

To learn how to bring out the best in people around him, and, organizationally, how to focus the resulting energy, motivation, creativity, and awareness on getting things done effectively and accomplishing missions.

His breakthrough experiences as a manager and executive at HP led him to found Enlightened Leadership Solutions, Inc. (ELS) in 1987 to formalize the ongoing learning and share it with the world.

His first book, "Enlightened Leadership: Getting to the *Heart* of Change," was a major best-seller that he co-authored with Doug

Krug. It continues to sell today through Simon & Schuster, as well as various ebook formats. It launched ELS as a worldwide venture, eventually impacting business leaders and their organizations/families from 68 countries.

Ed's forte has always been that of taking learnings from many sources and integrating them in new ways that provide breakthrough solutions to complex challenges. That is definitely the case with this work.

His recent understanding and experience of the power of consciousness shifts for business leaders and their influence is what led him to this current breakthrough work. While it fits others as well as organizational leaders, his focus is there because of the potential of using their leverage to make a much bigger difference to so many more people, including their organizations and families, too.

Mr. Oakley can be reached at 1-303-729-0540 during normal office hours in Denver, Colorado.

Where to Find More Information

The first thing you should do is register so we can let you know when Part 2 and Part 3 books are available. We'll also update data, perspectives and additional ideas about the material in each book. You'll get to all that through this registration page:

Register here:

http://www.enleadership.com/breakthrough/shift/

We'd like to invite you to join the conversation, as we hope soon to create an opportunity on the website to facilitate people sharing experiences with each other. Our team members will contribute, too.

To your breakthrough in consciousness and all the personal and professional benefits that offers you! We would love to hear from you.

The Enlightened Leadership Team
Contact us at 1-303-729-0540 or contactus@enleadership.com. Office hours are generally 9am-5pm Mountain Time.

Other books by Ed Oakley:

*Enlightened Leadership:
Getting to the Heart of Change*

*Be a Trusted Leader:
Accelerate Your Influence Now!*

*Shift Consciousness, Change Everything,
Parts 2 and 3*